Counting Balloons

by Ljiljana Rylands

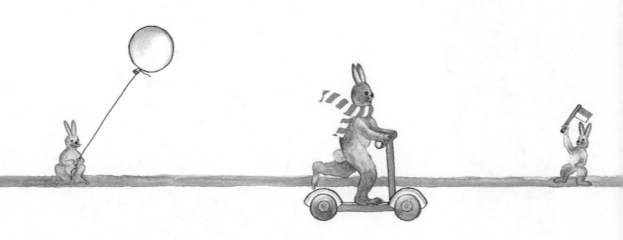

Published by McClanahan Book Company, Inc.

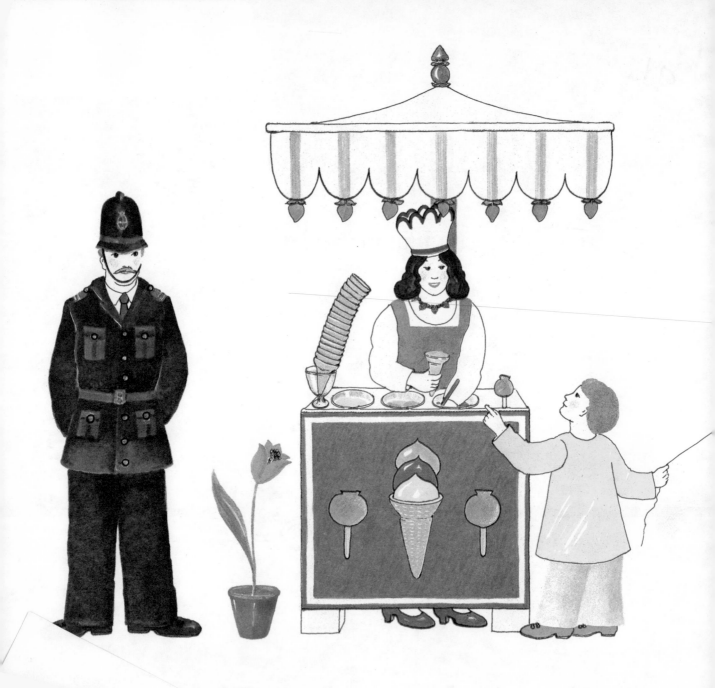

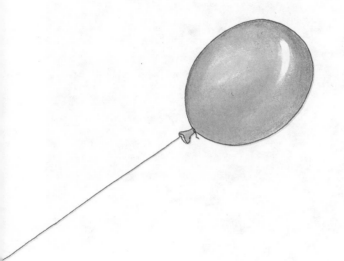

1 one

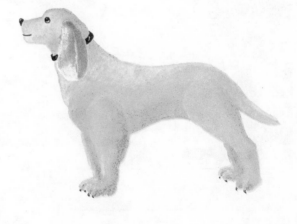

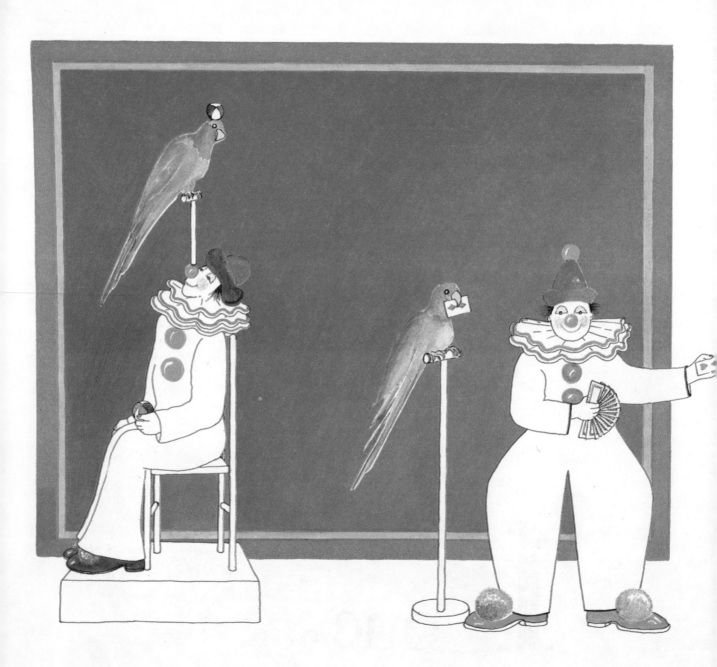

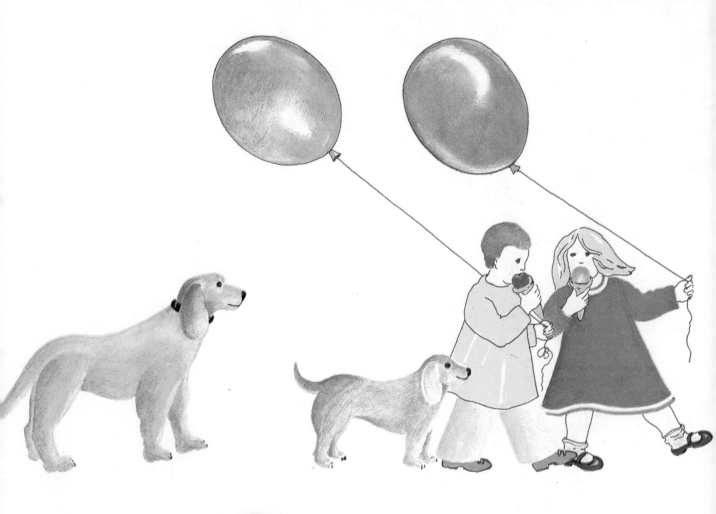

2 two

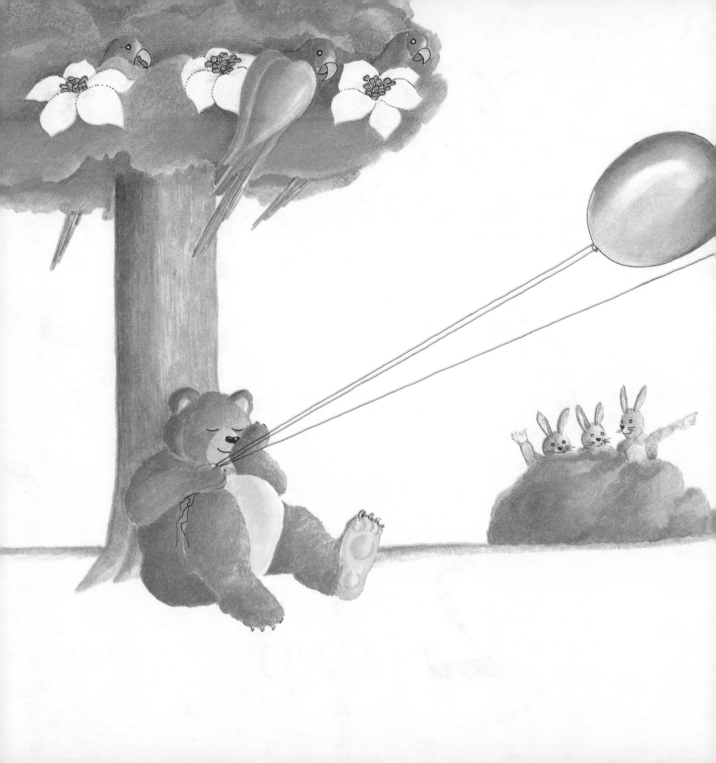

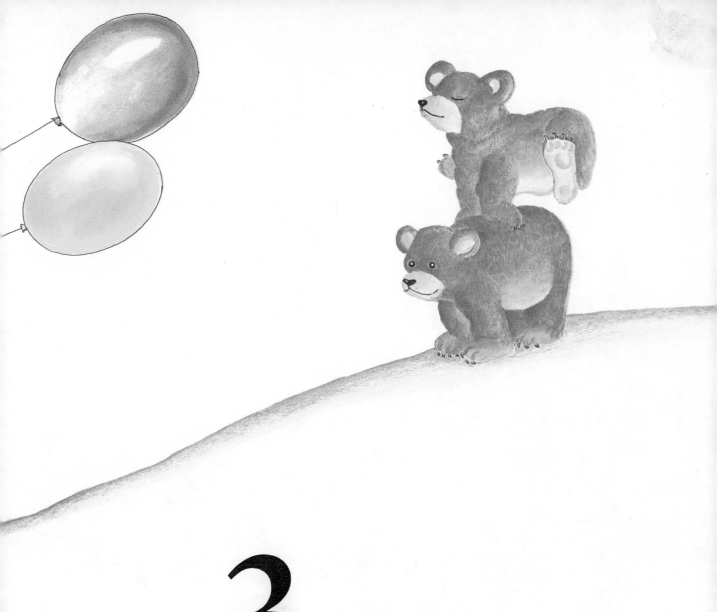

3 three

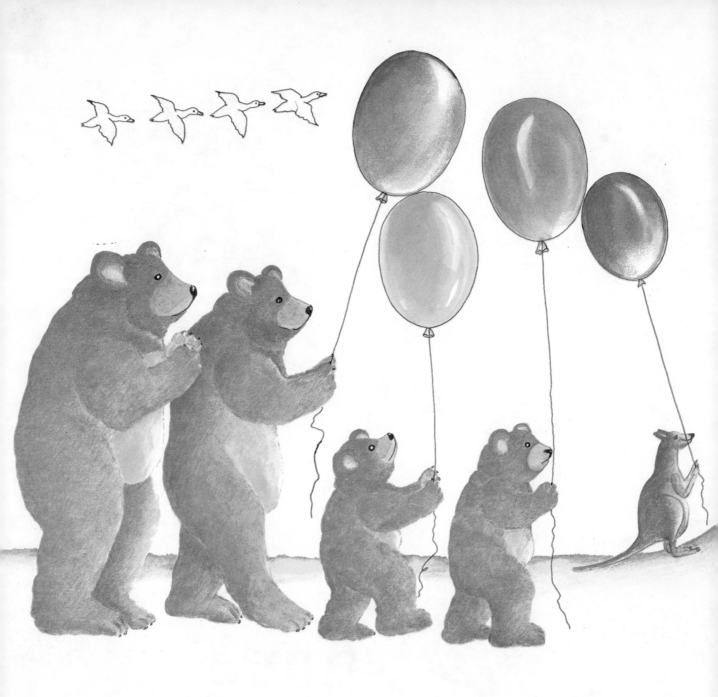

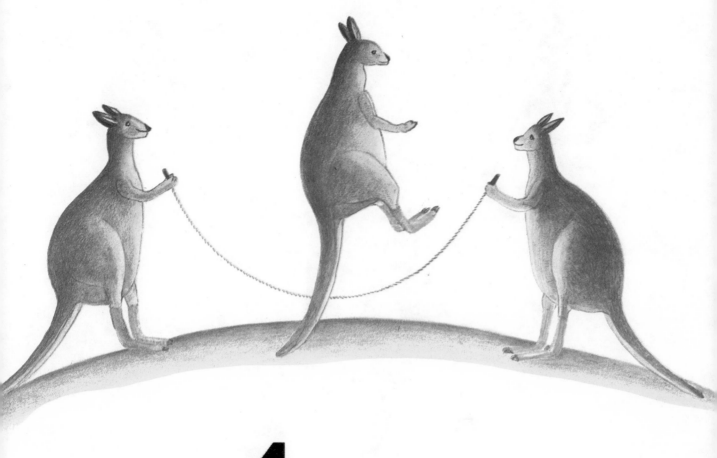

4 four

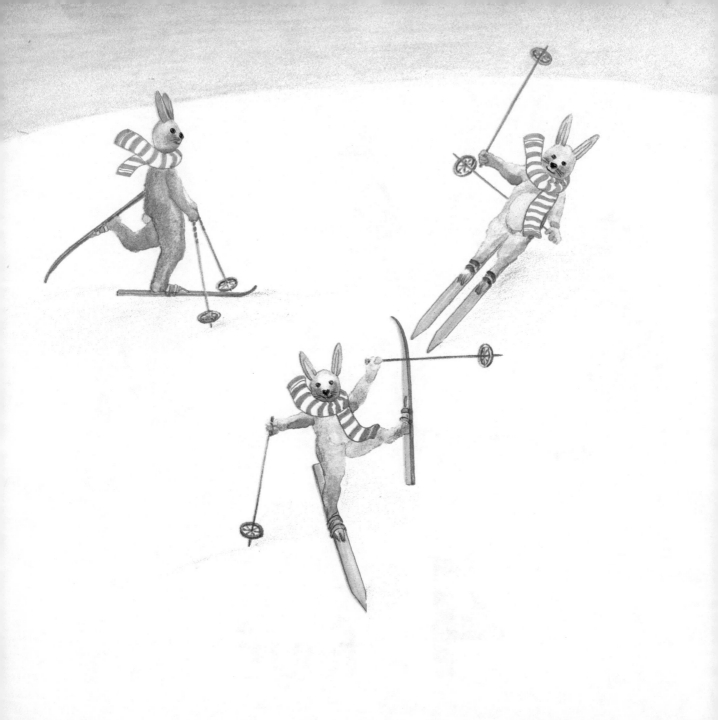

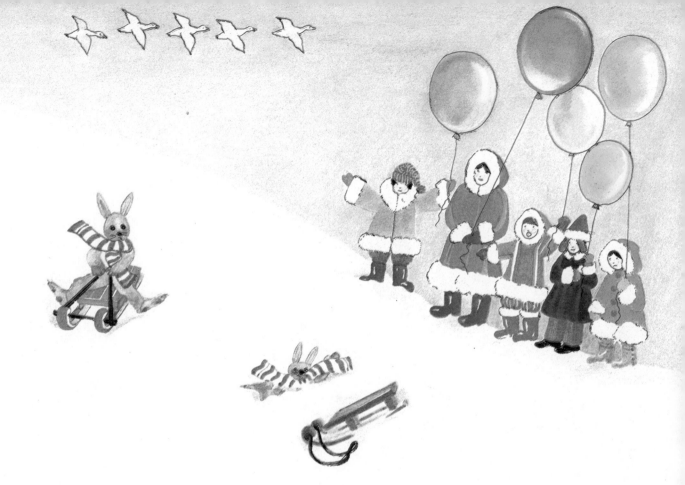

5 five

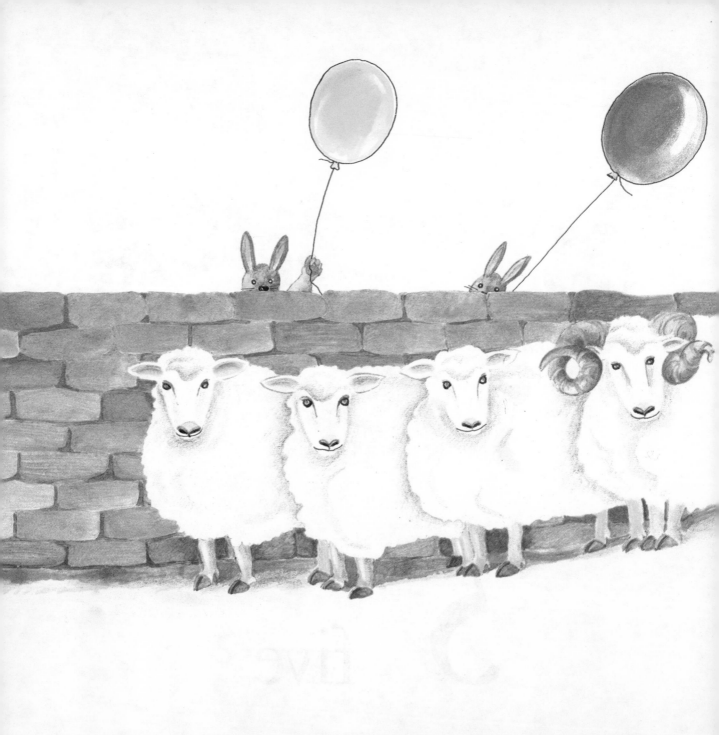

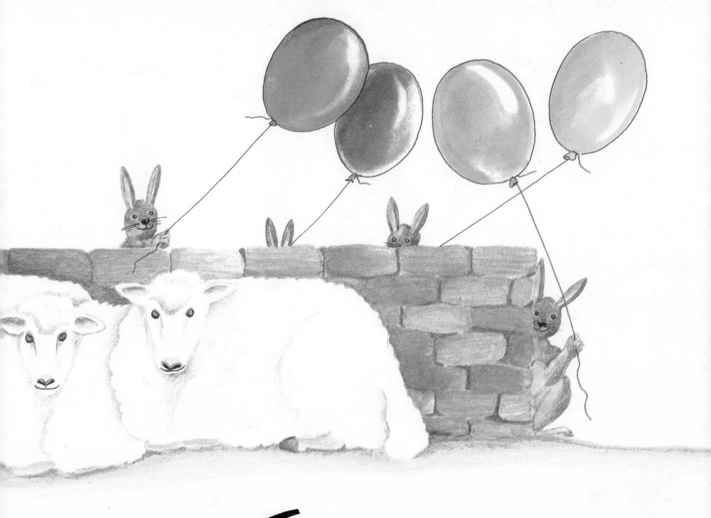

6 six

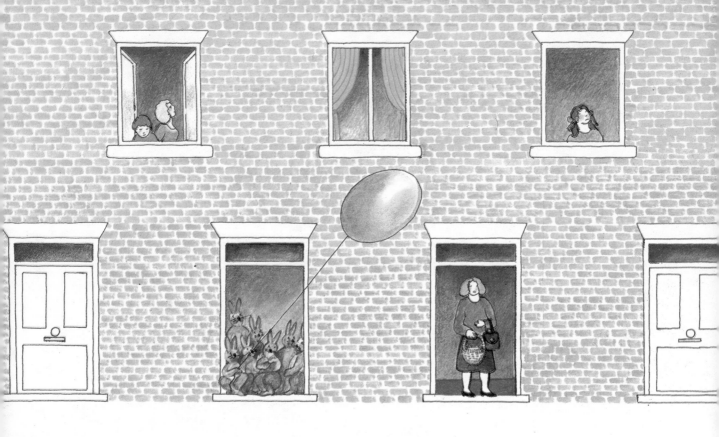

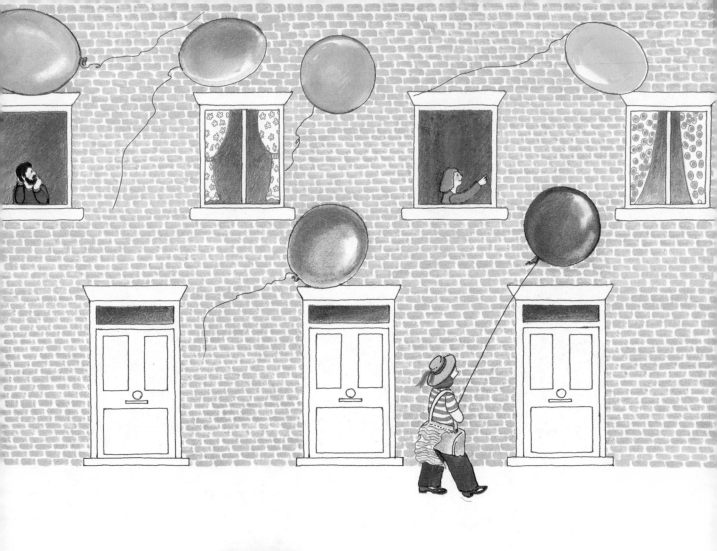

7 seven

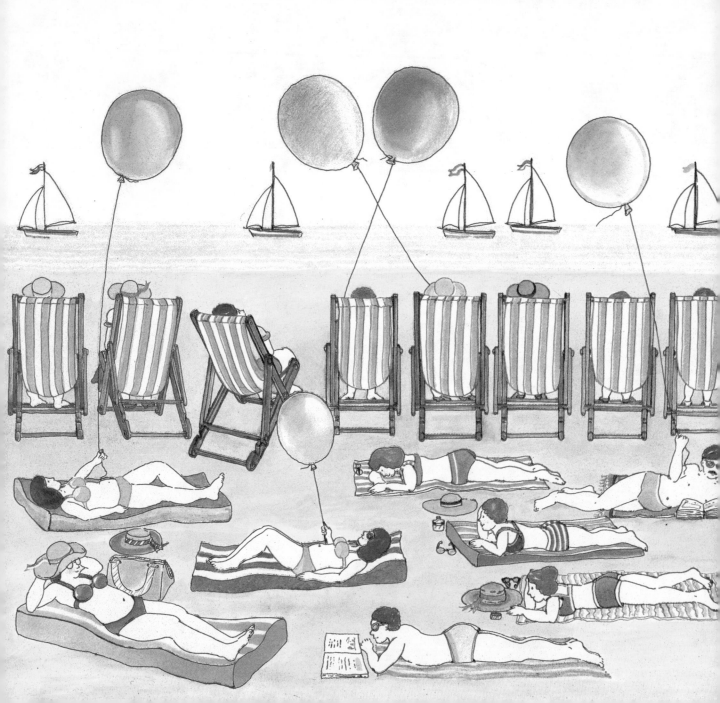

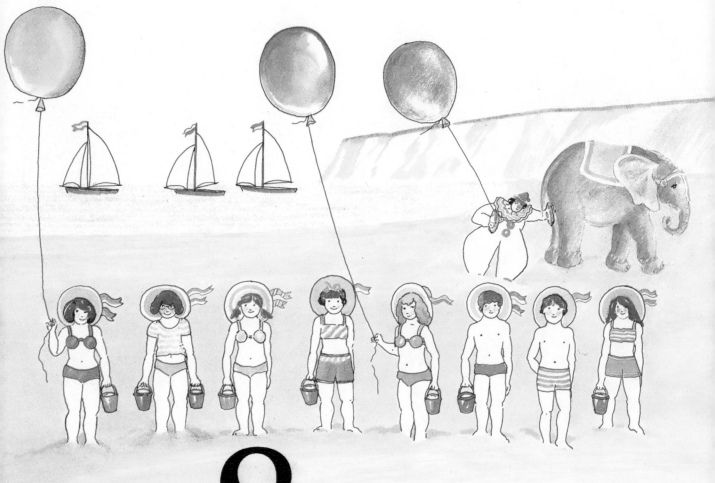

8 eight

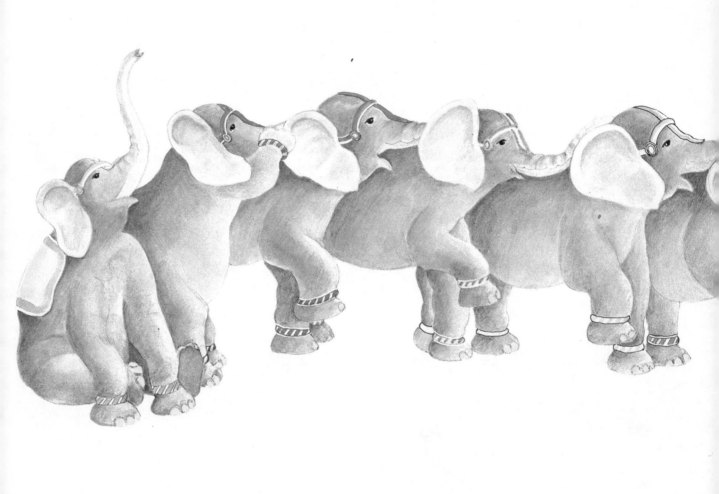

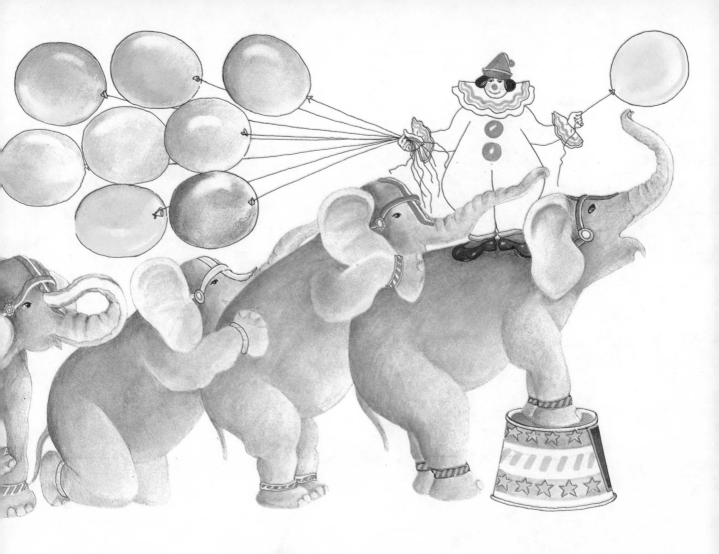

9 nine

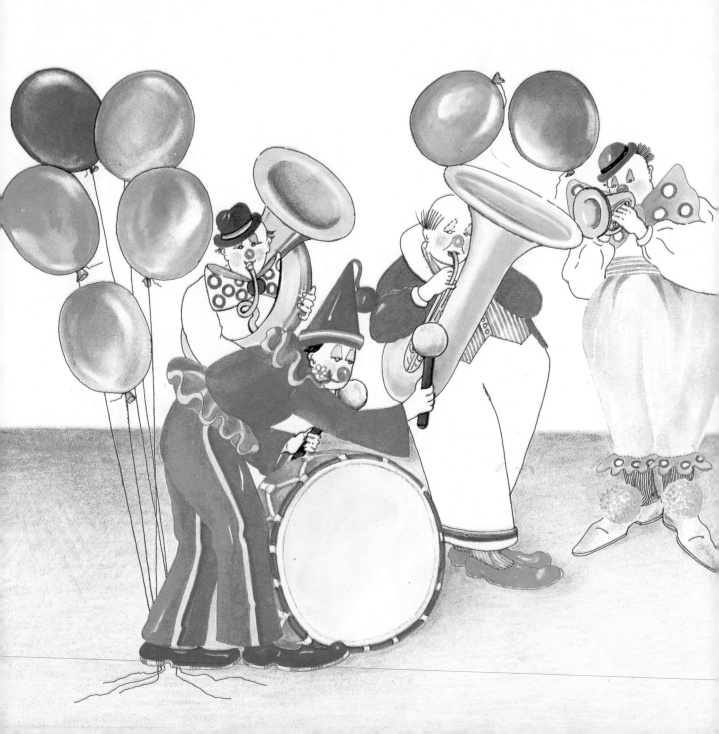

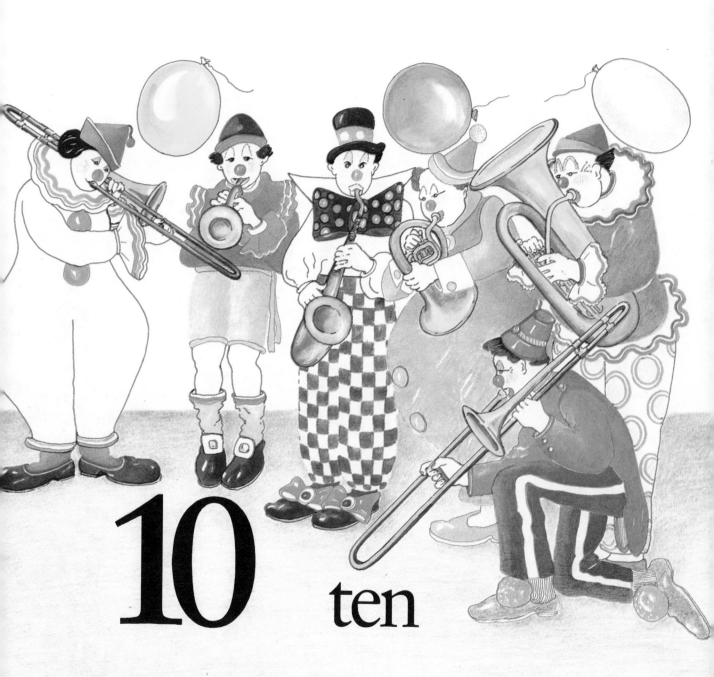

10 ten

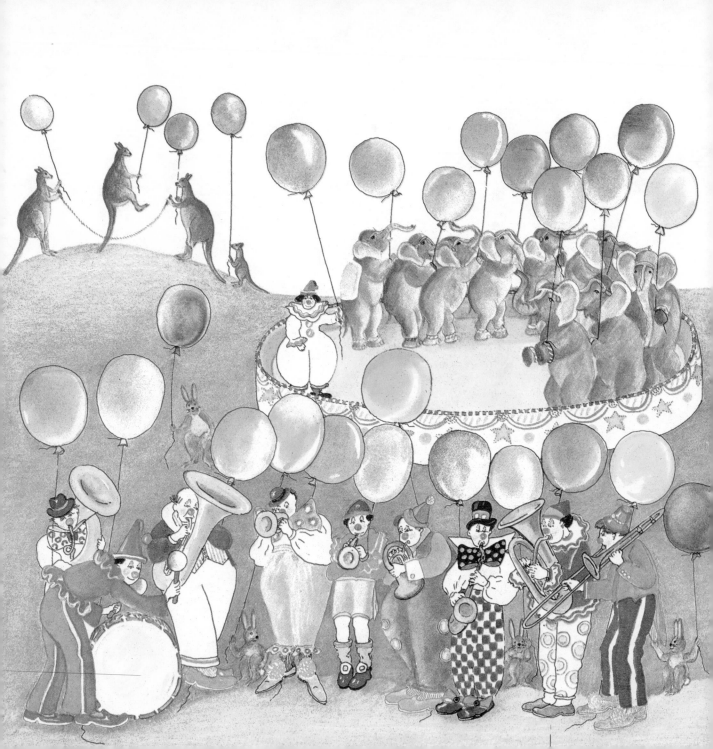

How many balloons can you count here?

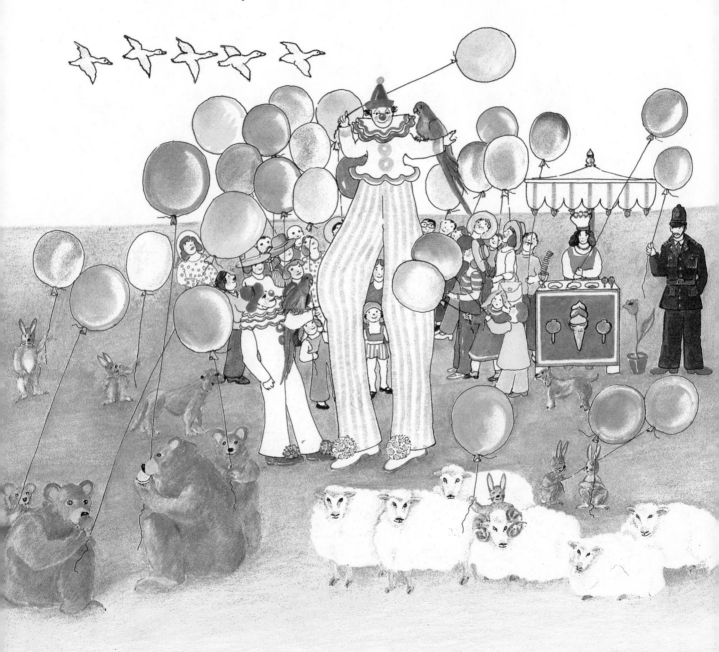

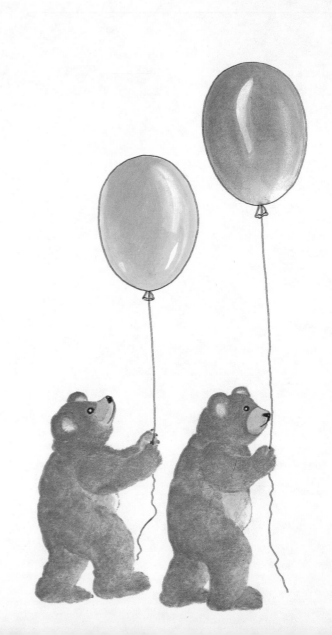